CREDIT SCORING SECRETS

How To Raise Your Credit Score

100 Points In 100 Days

© Copyright 2018 by James L. Paris, LLC

How Anyone Can Quickly Raise Their Credit Score

If you are a regular visitor to my website, you may already be aware that in 2002 I was the victim of an embezzlement scheme. After losing my financial planning business, my home, cars, and virtually all of my possessions, I had to start over. I believe that God allows us to go through difficult times for a reason. I sincerely believe that I am now wiser and even more equipped to help people with their finances than ever before. This report is about credit scoring; a topic I knew far less about than I thought. Over the years in my public appearances, probably no other single topic has been raised more often than credit. I guess that makes sense, since credit is really a part of everything we do with our finances. Not only is credit a factor when a person seeks a loan or a credit card, credit is now used by human resource departments to make hiring decisions. Although very controversial, credit is also a major factor in determining insurance rates as well. In Florida, where I live, bad credit can mean a 30% increase in the cost of your insurance! This really hits your pocketbook when you consider how expensive insurance already is.

For many years, I also worked in the real estate and mortgage industries. Although I regularly dealt with the issue of real estate and mortgages in my financial planning practice, the time I spent working *directly* in these areas provided me with an unbelievable education, including some explosive information that I am ready to share here.

Credit scoring is something that most people have heard about, but few people understand. I have found that when people have some basic information on a subject, they can be very difficult to teach (hence the saying, *"A little bit of knowledge can be dangerous"*). An example of this arose when a man once came to my mortgage office seeking advice on raising his credit score so that he could obtain a mortgage. I had spent nearly an hour reviewing his credit and making notes prior to his arrival. He was a mountain of a man, probably 6' 4" and 250 pounds. As I attempted to go over his credit file and offer him my advice, he continually interrupted me by saying, "I know." This went on for about twenty minutes and I politely ended our meeting without being able to really give him much help. About three months later, he returned to my office eager to have me check his credit report. As he waited patiently, with a big grin on his face, I had to ask him what he had done and why he was so excited to see his credit report. He told me, "Just pull it up and you will see." I did, and the results were shocking to me and devastating to this young man.

I shared with him that his credit score had dropped about one hundred points since his last visit. This huge guy started to cry in my office. At this point, I was confused and very nervous about the prospect of this guy starting to turn over desks and file cabinets out of anger. I asked him to share with me what he had done since we last met. He explained that with money from his parents, and several thousand dollars borrowed from his retirement plan, he paid off all of his bad debts and credit cards (and closed them). While still very upset, he asked me, "Are you saying that because I did this, I won't be able to get approved to buy a house now?" The answer was yes, at least for the time being. This story really exemplifies the kind of crazy scenarios that I have witnessed over the last several years. It was a whole new experience to me to actually review thousands of credit reports and witness firsthand the cause and effect of people's actions on their scores. **Doing what you might think is *right*, could actually destroy your credit.** I will address later in this book why paying off some bad debts may not be a good idea and how this could even make your score lower, as in the story above.

Why Credit Scoring?

The idea of using a mathematical measurement of person's credit file makes sense at some level. We use numbers to measure grades in school, so why not credit? Most young people today have no memory of relationship-based lending. Some readers of this book may remember visiting their local bank to apply for a mortgage or auto loan and discussing their loan with a *person*, perhaps someone with whom they had a long-established banking relationship. Even such considerations as dressing up and presenting yourself appropriately were all recognized as a large part of getting an approval in the person-to person process. Applying for a loan may have at one time been a close cousin to applying for a job. Now, credit decisions are boiled down to a three digit number and usually made by a computer, not a human. **While converting the subjective world of *good and bad credit* into a number is innovative and potentially very useful, it also creates**

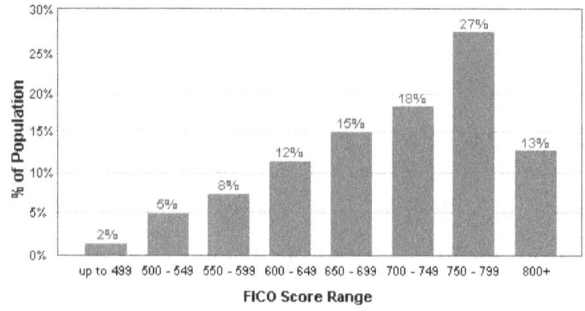

Chart Source: Bankrate.com

a large number of challenges. Who decides how these scores are calculated? What type of credit behavior constitutes good credit and is deserving of a high score? What type of credit behavior constitutes bad credit?

Credit Scores Nationwide

Scores range between 350 (extremely high risk) and 850 (extremely low risk). Here is a breakdown of the distribution of scores for the American population:

What Is Good Credit?

The answer to this question would probably vary widely, depending on who was answering and what type of lending was involved. Based on my experience in originating mortgage loans, **I would have to say that the dividing point between good and subpar credit would be at about a 640 score.** Below a 640 is most likely going to be treated as less than favorable credit, and above a 640 would be good or strong credit. This all occurs, of course, in varying degrees. A 639 is not much worse than a 640, so don't get caught up in believing that there is something magical about the number 640. Obviously, if you are below a 640, the closer you get to that level, the better chance you have at being viewed as at least "B" credit vs. a "C" or "D."

Why Are My Three Credit Scores Different?

Your credit scores will vary between each of the three bureaus for two reasons. First, each bureau has different data on you. Not all of your accounts are going to report to all three bureaus and even in the cases where they do, they may have slightly or even dramatically different data in your file on behalf of the very same account. How this happens, I don't really know for sure, other than to guess that when any two large organizations share data there are likely going to be mistakes and anomalies in this massive data transfer. The second reason that your scores are going to vary between the three bureaus is that each bureau calculates scores differently. While the process is *not exactly the same*, it is close enough to not make that big of a disparity in point totals. If I find that a client has a considerably different score with one bureau vs.

the other two, it is almost always related to a significant dissimilarity in the information that is on file. A common example of this would be a collection account that is only reported to one of the three bureaus. The two bureaus that have not received this information have no knowledge of it and it will not affect your score with them.

The Importance of Maintaining Good Credit With All Three Bureaus

In the mortgage business, *all three credit scores* are taken into consideration. This requires retrieving what is known as a "tri-merged" credit report. With three scores to work with, we use the *middle* of the three. This is not an *average of the three*, but the middle of the three. As an example, if someone had a 750, 640, and a 639, the middle score would be a **640**. This would definitely be lower than the average of the three, which would be a 676. **I don't know why the middle score is used, but that is the system in mortgage lending. Since you won't know which score is going to come up as your middle score, you need to be sure and maintain good scores at all three bureaus.** Also, there will be many situations where a credit score from only one bureau will be considered. In these instances, you may be sunk if it happens to be the one bureau that you have not been keeping close tabs on. This is an important consideration, as many individuals rely on information from only one bureau in evaluating their own credit status.

A Review Of The Fair Credit Reporting Act & Your Credit Rights

While this report will be focused only on credit scoring, I thought it would be useful to briefly review the basic credit rights that we all have as a result of the Fair Credit Reporting Act.

The right to receive a free copy of your credit report when you are denied credit.

The right to have incorrect information removed from your credit report.

The right to have positive information added that may be missing.

The ability to add a 100 word statement to explain any derogatory information.

The right to remove any credit item that is older than 7 years (or bankruptcy 10 years).

The problem with many of these credit "rights" is that they really don't help us that much in the world of credit scoring. For example, adding a 100-word explanation to your credit report is a complete waste of time. This will have no bearing on your credit score and believe me, no one will read it. Older items (7 years or more), if not reporting currently, are really having no effect on your score either. A free copy of your credit report is really not that useful without also receiving your credit scores. In fact, **one bureau's report is completely useless without having the reports and scores from the other two bureaus along with it.** I will address the issue of removing negative items later in this book.

Getting A Glimpse Into the Mysterious World of Credit Scoring

While attending a mortgage broker conference several years ago, I was fortunate to be able to attend a seminar on credit scoring. The person presenting the seminar had been provided the information they were sharing directly from the credit bureaus. In fact, I don't know how much of this they were supposed to really pass along, but I took very good notes. I really did not expect to get very much out of the seminar, as I thought I already had a firm grasp on the issue of credit. **What I did not realize is that in the years that had passed since I had written my last book, credit scoring had really taken over as the primary means by** which credit decision were made. I was learning very quickly how little I really knew and understood about the new score-based credit world.

When You're In Someone Else's Ballpark, You Play by Their Rules

It would be fair to say that I don't agree with, nor do I like, many of the methods that are used in credit scoring. I don't plan to spend much time in this book addressing my disagreement with the methodology. **I have found in my individual client consultations, as well as in the seminars I teach on credit scoring, that people invest entirely too much energy in complaining about the current system.** I encourage you to take this information and use it to your advantage. For some clients, the only way that I could get them to focus their energy away from their disagreement with the system and on raising their own scores was to have them think of it as a game - *the credit scoring game*. **Imagine you are playing Monopoly or some other board game, and are simply working towards a goal of winning the game. This may help you immensely when you continue to read this report and begin to run across ideas that don't make sense to you and that don't fit into your current financial lifestyle.** One example of this I many times face with Christians is the issue of number of open credit accounts. For good reason, many Christian financial seminars and books warn against the dangers of credit cards. **Most of this teaching has led to people keeping just one or two open credit card accounts. This is good financial planning advice, but not good advice on building a credit score; more about that later.**

The Starting Point – Obtaining Your Credit Report

If you have not already done so, you should retrieve your credit report from one of the various online services. Be sure to obtain all three of your credit scores as well. Many of these offers will require that you sign up for credit monitoring. That is a very good idea, as it allows for your credit to be scrutinized on a daily basis, but you don't have to keep the credit monitoring if you don't opt to pay for that service. It is true that you can order your reports directly from the credit bureaus for free one time per year, but these free reports don't include the scores and, honestly, that is the most important piece of information you need to see.

What Are Your Real Credit Scores?

As a disclaimer, you should know that the scores you purchase from any of the major services are not your *real credit scores*. It is still worth getting them, though, as they represent an approximation of your score (+/- about 25 points). **I don't know why the scores provided to consumers are different from the scores that appear on a real credit report, but they are.** I used to have clients come into my office with their credit report and scores in hand, and they never match up with the scores I would get when pulling up reports from the credit bureaus directly. **Mortgage companies have the ability to access these commercial-level reports, which are much more comprehensive than the reports available directly to the public.** Again, this is another issue we can all wonder about. Why can't a person get the same scores that a lender will get? It doesn't seem fair, but that is the way the system is currently operating.

In Order To Win The Credit Game, You Must Have Credit!

Many a client has said to me, "I don't believe in credit" while sitting in my office applying for a mortgage (isn't a mortgage credit?). Upon further clarification, they meant credit cards and revolving types of credit. As a result, they had not one credit card. Perhaps a good thing, you might be thinking. Credit cards are bad, right? Well, this is where the credit game begins. While we might all agree that paying cash is a better financial planning option than using credit, having *no* open credit cards will destroy your credit score. **In order to achieve a high credit score, you will most likely need to have a minimum of four open revolving credit card accounts.**

Please note that I did not suggest that you had to use these cards or run up high balances on them. In fact, the lower your balances, the more points you will gain. You might be asking, "How do I get four credit card accounts if I have bad credit?" If you go to Christian Money.com, you will find a number of secured credit card options available to you. Secured credit cards require a deposit equal to the amount of credit they extend to you. **Since the debt is secured, low credit scores should not stop you from obtaining these cards.**

30% Of Score Is Based On Credit Card Balances vs. Available Credit

If you want to get some quick and easy points, lowering your credit

card balances is the way to go. The ideal scenario is to never use more than 35% of the available credit you have on any credit or revolving credit line. For clarification, I am only addressing *revolving accounts* at this point ("R" accounts). This does not apply to mortgages, auto loans, and other installment type debt. **For example, if you surf over to Christian Money.com and pick up four secured credit cards with $300 lines of credit on each and then max them out, <u>you will lose points!</u> In fact, you will likely have a lower score than the one you had before you started this whole project.** Some people absolutely cannot help themselves, however. I have had clients come into my office, go out and get the secured cards as I instructed, and then two months later they had nearly reached the credit limit on all of the cards. Believe me I have heard every story you can imagine, such as, "We had no choice - it was Christmas" or, "We needed new tires for the car." **I guess this is why the credit scoring people think their system is infallible - even when a person knows the formula, he still can't help going back to his old habits.**

One other issue that you should be aware of is that we don't know what day of the month that a balance on a particular credit card may be reported to the credit bureau. **As a result, in order to follow my 35% rule, <u>you can never go above 35% of the available balance at any time during the month</u>.**

I had a client who opened several secured credit card accounts and then began using them on her various business trips. On the 1st of every month, she would pay off the entire balance on each card with the reimbursements she received from her company. Nevertheless, her credit score tanked because all of the cards were *reporting the balances toward the last ten days of the month*. In her mind she was carrying zero balances, but that was not how the credit scoring system was grading these accounts. For most people, the quickest and easiest way to raise their credit score is to reduce the balances on revolving accounts.

A revolving account is a credit line that allows you to pay down the balance and then borrow again up to the entirety of the credit line. This is in contrast to an installment loan (auto loans are an example of this type of account) that has a fixed payment and a fixed payment period (reported on your credit file as an "I" account). After the balance is reduced, you do not have the privilege to borrow more money.

Revolving accounts (reported on your credit file as "R" accounts) are the only accounts subject to scoring that's based on balance vs. available credit (debt utilization ratio). Also, another type of installment loan, one secured by real estate, is reported as an "M" account ("M" for mortgage).

How To Contact The Credit Bureaus

Throughout this report, I will make suggestions regarding contacting the credit bureaus about various inaccuracies in your credit file. Unlike the old days, you can now contact the credit bureaus online and through various toll-free numbers. **I have still found the most efficient method for contacting the credit bureaus is in writing. It is my theory that this is the most difficult format for them to deal with; accordingly, you are a "squeakier wheel" when mailing in your complaint.** If you want to try to work with them by phone and/or the Internet, that is up to you, but with these methods, getting rid of you is a simple click of the delete button or hanging up the phone. **Good old-fashioned letter writing seems to yield the best results. Important: When writing to the credit bureau, always include your Social Security Number, current address, sign your letter, and include copies of at least two forms of** identification (that must match your current residence address). It would not hurt to also include a copy of a recent utility bill with your current address as well (this is starting to become a regular item that they ask for). You can make a copy of your driver's license and a voter ID card, or other government issued ID. **If you don't take the time to do this, your letter will be returned, and this will be their excuse why your inquiry can't be processed.** Also, remember when you correspond with the credit bureau, you must communicate on behalf of yourself only. **If you are married, this means that you and your spouse will need to send separate letters addressing your individual issues. Do not send letters addressing the issues of more than one person, or even combine these letters in the same envelope. If you don't take the time to follow the above guidelines, you will spend weeks seeing your letters returned with no action.**

What To Do If The Credit Bureau Does Not Live Up To Their Obligations

You can certainly fire off a letter of complaint to the attorney general of your state and to the Federal Trade Commission; that may make you feel better but may not really get you what you want – namely, your credit file updated. Note that I have used a service called Pre Paid Legal, both on behalf of myself as well as recommending this to my clients. How the service works is that for a monthly membership cost of about $25 (varies by state), you join a legal plan that allows you to access attorneys. Under the basic plan, one of the benefits is unlimited phone consultations and letter writing on your behalf to resolve legal problems. **If you are willing to spend the $25 a month for a few months, you can have the lawyers dispute your credit report items for you. This really works and will get things removed and/or updated very quickly.** I guess when the credit bureaus go through their stacks of mail, the letters from law firms get opened first.

http://DefendYourRights.US (Note: I am also a member of their affiliate program).

Be Sure You Are Getting The Points For Your Low Balance

Another fascinating irregularity about the credit scoring system is that occasionally a credit card issuer will not report to the bureaus the available credit on a card and only post the *current balance* and the *highest balance*. Capital One, at one time, was known for doing this. When you review your credit report, you will notice the amount of your current balance and in the very next column, your total available credit. For example, I may have a card with a total available credit of $500 and a current balance of $150. In this scenario, I am only using 30% of my available credit, so this should give me plenty of points, right? **The problem is that some credit card companies only report your <u>highest balance and *not* your total available credit</u>. To combat this, all that is necessary is to max out the card as soon as you get it, and then pay it off right away.** I have done this myself and it is very easy. Most of these cards allow a cash advance. If it is a $500 card, take a $500 cash advance and then immediately deposit that into your checking account and send that money to the credit card company. Keep in mind <u>that you do not have do this unless you happen to notice that they are not reporting your total available credit.</u>

Installment Loans ("I") Accounts

Ten percent of your credit score is based on type and mixture of credit accounts. I have found that **to achieve the best results, you should have at least one open installment account.** To review, an installment account is not the same as a credit card or revolving account; an installment account begins with a set balance and a fixed payment that does not change, nor can you borrow back any amount you have already paid back. This account will have an "I" next to it on your credit report. A common example of an installment debt would be an auto loan**. If you don't have an auto loan or at least one installment loan, you need to establish one.** The easiest way to do this is to go to a local bank or credit union and ask them if they offer small secured loans for the purpose of rebuilding credit. There is a local credit union here in Daytona Beach, Florida that I use frequently for this. My clients would go in and open up a $300 savings account and then take a $300 installment loan, using the savings account as collateral. Of course, everyone is approved as this is a no-risk transaction for the credit union. Under this arrangement, the client makes a $50 monthly payment for six months and then is entitled to receive back the $300 they have on deposit. I usually recommend not taking the $300 back out of savings, but initiating another loan and doing this over and over again. Talk about points - you will really score big with this strategy. I have had clients get 50 or more points just from having one installment loan in good standing with a credit union.

You don't want another credit card, so don't get confused and walk

out with a credit card. **If you are given a credit card, this is not an installment loan and you have just opened another revolving account.**

How To Deal With Collection Accounts and Other "Bad Credit" Items

Thirty-five percent of your overall credit score is based on what is loosely called "payment history." This encompasses a lot of factors beyond making your payments on a timely basis. This would also include public record items such as tax liens, bankruptcies, and foreclosures, as well as any accounts you may have in collection (more on public record items later). Collection accounts are really a mystery to me. A question I have asked over the years is why organizations are allowed to report bad credit if they don't also report good credit**. For example, if you pay your utilities on time every month for ten years, you will never see that on your credit report nor will you receive any benefit or points for having made these timely payments.** Now, if you move and, by mistake, end up with a $10 unpaid balance, you can be sure that within a matter of weeks that unpaid balance will be reflected in your credit file. Furthermore, you will likely lose quite a few points for having a recently-filed collection account in your record. I have suggested in my seminars that there should be a law which requires any organization that wants the privilege of reporting bad credit to also have the responsibility to report good credit, as well. Sounds reasonable, right? Maybe something for us all to write Congress about.

One of the shocking things that I learned in my research into credit scoring is that scores are based almost entirely on the data that has been reported in your file during the last 12 to 18 months. Anything older than 18 months has such little bearing on your score that you might as well not even be concerned about it. The good news about this is that even though you may have been through a very difficult financial situation causing you to have late payments, collections, etc… it will only take a year to 18 months to have very strong credit again. The bad news is that even if you have paid your bills perfectly on time for years and years, perhaps for as long as a decade, you can lose your good credit very quickly. The credit scoring models, designed to predict your future ability to make your payments on time, are based on the premise that your most recent financial history is the single, biggest factor of this prediction.

To Pay Or Not Pay A Collection Account

As illustrated in the story at the beginning of this report, <u>many times paying a bad debt will lower, not raise, your credit score.</u> Based on the last time a collection item was reported on your credit file, you will have to decide if it is a priority to pay or not. As a Christian, I have to insert a big disclaimer here. **I am not saying that you should avoid paying your debts. In fact, the best time to try and resolve a debt is before it ends up with a collector.** This is especially true in the case of department store credit cards, where they will typically agree to delete negative information (or the account altogether) if you clear up any past due balance you have. My recommendations here are strictly based on achieving the quickest increase in your score. If you are in the process of applying for a mortgage or need to achieve the highest score possible for something you are working on now, you can follow these strategies and then later go back and work on old, non-reporting debts (after you have obtained your mortgage, or otherwise achieved your short term objective). **With that in mind, the most important factor in determining whether or not to pay a collection (for credit scoring purposes only) is the date that it last reported to the credit bureau.**

This is extremely important, so I want to be sure that you completely understand the concept.

Your credit report may be twenty pages long and have dozens of accounts listed. Each account listed contains the date that it was last reported to the credit bureau. **Therefore, you cannot conclude that if it is simply on your report that it has just reported fresh data this last month. <u>You must take the time to go through each collection account and determine the date it last reported to the bureau. If the account last reported more than 12 to 18 months ago, you will most likely lower your score if you pay it off.</u> In my seminars, I call *this waking up the dead*.** Once an old collection account is contacted, they will begin to report fresh data on you to the bureau. Even if the fresh data reported is a "paid collection" (you pay the debt in full or settle it), it is still going to cost you points, since this is considered a negative account for credit scoring purposes (less negative than an unpaid collection, to be sure, but negative nonetheless). **Due to this anomaly in the credit scoring system, and while our immediate goal is point accumulation, we must focus only on those collection accounts that have reported fresh data to the bureaus during the last 12 to 18 months.**

Settling Collection Accounts

Once you have determined which collection accounts have been reporting fresh data to the credit bureaus, you now have your list of accounts to consider settling. Another factor to weigh is the amount of money involved in the collection. What I found in my mortgage business was that **settling smaller collection accounts seems to have about the same impact as settling larger accounts.** Again, this is not something that anyone would expect to be the case. I think it would only be common sense to think that a large collection is more damaging than a small collection, but that does not seem to be how the game is played. **As a result, we have seen people settle a $10 dental bill and gain the same number of points as those who settle a collection account for several hundreds of dollars.** At some level, the credit scoring algorithm seems to count all bad accounts similarly, regardless of the amounts of money involved.

Settling a collection account can be tricky. First, you have to get in touch with the collector. Many times, the collector's phone number will appear on the credit report along with the negative information they are reporting. In some instances, you will have to use the Internet or other resources to track down a collector. Once you make contact with the collector, you should ask them to send you something to establish that the debt they are collecting is legitimate (should you have any doubts about whether you really owe it or not). There should be some kind of paper trail, like a service contract you signed or something else establishing that you owe the debt in the first place. Once you feel comfortable that the collector is actually collecting on a valid debt, then the negotiations can begin. **Most collection account balances represent 3 to 5 times the amount of the original debt. This is typically due to late fees, penalties, interest, etc…. As a result, the original amount of the debt may only represent 20 to 25 percent of what is now in collections.** You should also understand that most collection firms acquire this debt for 5 to 10% of the gross amount. As an example, a $1,000 collection account may be purchased for as little as $50 to $100 by a collector. Once you understand the numbers here, you may start to see why it is possible to negotiate a settlement for far less that 100% of the amount in play. **From my experience in assisting hundreds of clients, settlement discussions should start at about 30% and end up being settled for about 50% of the total amount.** Again, this is probably far more than you owed to begin with, but is still a sum that's a lot less than what you legally owe at the time you first hear from the collection agency, and is also an amount that will allow the collector to make a good return on his investment (a win-win). **Once you reach a settlement with the collector, you should not pay them until they provide a settlement letter which completely releases you from the debt for the amount agreed on (conditional on receiving your payment in the agreed amount).**

While engaging in your settlement efforts, be very careful what information you provide to the debt collector. If you provide them your work phone number, or current home phone number, you may get hammered with collection calls if you ultimately can't amicably settle your debt with them. **You should never pay a collector with a credit card or give them your checking account number. Pay with a money order, and only after receiving the settlement letter.** I have had several clients call me and ask what to do if the collector won't give them a settlement letter. Answer: Don't pay them. Most of the time, as soon as they realize that you will not make the payment without a settlement letter, you will quickly get one. If you do make a payment without the settlement letter, you really have no recourse to be able to prove that you have a valid settlement.

What To Do If A Debt Remains After You Have Settled It

At this point, you will be relying on the paper trail that you have created. By the way, you should keep the proof of your settled debt for at least 3 to 4 years, just in case the item pops back up on your credit report down the road. I always recommend that any letter sent to the credit bureaus be sent certified mail with return receipt.

Here is an example letter:

To whom it may concern:

I entered into a settlement agreement with ABC Debt Collection. As you will see from the enclosed documentation, they agreed in writing to a settlement on this account for $201. I have also enclosed a copy of the money order proving that this amount was paid to them as agreed. Therefore, I am requesting that this account be either deleted or reported as paid with a 0 balance.

Thank You

Is It Possible To Get Collection Items Completely Deleted

Some companies may agree to delete a settled account completely from your report, but most will not. There are federal laws dealing with debt collection that a collector may be concerned about in making this kind of bargain - if they offer to remove a negative item altogether after payment, it may be interpreted as collecting a debt through extortionate means (a threatening manner). Therefore, most often the collection status will be changed to *paid collection* and the balance will be updated to 0. **If you are able to get a debt collector to remove the account completely after payment, that is a home run.** One technique that I have seen work is the use of this type of settlement letter (below).

Dear Customer Service:

Enclosed is my check for $201, which represents payment in full for account #xxxxxxx.

By accepting this payment and depositing the enclosed check, you agree to delete all derogatory information being reported about this account.

Thank You

Using a letter like this will not guarantee a complete deletion, but it may be used as leverage to get the credit bureau to remove the account if the original creditor does not. It is also necessary to write 'payment in full' in the memo portion of the check as well.

Collection Accounts and Other Debts After Bankruptcy

A large part of my mortgage practice was dedicated to helping people obtain mortgages after bankruptcy. Up until the beginning of 2007, we had lenders willing to make zero down loans to individual just one day after the discharge of their bankruptcy. One of the requirements was a modest 580 middle credit score, but, that said, most people just out of bankruptcy, do not have a 580 score. One of my strategies to get these clients quick points was to help them to open up several new credit accounts and make a couple of on-time payments. The other issue was to get all of the items that were discharged in their bankruptcy zeroed out on their credit file, or deleted altogether. Oddly enough, I had clients come to my office years after the discharge of their bankruptcies and saw that most of their "discharged" debts were still listed in their credit files as unpaid. This is another major flaw in the credit reporting system. Although the credit bureaus are very quick to pick up a bankruptcy, foreclosure, or other public record filing and add it to a credit file, there is no system in place to deal with discharged debts. In legal terms, once your bankruptcy is over and you receive your discharge letter from the court, you no longer legally owe the debts included in the bankruptcy. That being said, there is no process by which anyone changes the status of these debts with the credit bureau. The court will not do it, your lawyer is not going to do it, and the credit bureau has no system to handle this. Thus, you must write a letter to each of the three credit bureaus, including a list of the debts from your bankruptcy filing, and include a copy of your discharge letter and schedule or creditors. What you are requesting is that all debts that were discharged in your bankruptcy be updated accordingly.

How this works is that a debt item balance will go to 0, and the phrase "included in bankruptcy" will be added. **If the balance is not 0, it is still going to drag your score down significantly. It is not enough to just get "included in bankruptcy" added to the account; the balance owed must be changed to 0.** If you don't include your bankruptcy schedule of creditors and your discharge letter when writing to the credit bureau, be prepared to receive everything back in about 30 days with no action taken. I have been through this countless times with clients. Save yourself a lot of time and put together a complete package.

Public Record Items

By receiving data from the courts and from other public records sources throughout the country, the credit bureau picks up a number of public record filings. These include bankruptcies, foreclosures, judgments, tax liens, unpaid child support, as well as a host of other items. A public record notation will affect your credit very similarly to collection accounts. For example, once a bankruptcy is added, it is viewed as negative and points are subtracted, and once the bankruptcy is discharged, its effect begins to wane. The more time that passes from the date of discharge, the less it will weigh on your overall score. The point is that having public records items on your credit is not the kiss of death. What is important is to be sure that the information is being reported *correctly* and that you "close out" the item as soon as is practical. By all means, challenge the item if any aspect of it is in error. Public record items can, on occasion, be easy to have deleted since they are not as easy to verify as collection accounts.

The Truth About Inquiries

An inquiry is registered with the credit bureaus each time your credit is ordered by a potential credit grantor. The most that inquiries can weigh on your score is 10%. I cannot begin to tell you how paranoid clients would become about me checking their credit, as they erroneously believed that they were going to lose dozens of points by me doing so. If someone wants a mortgage, the complete credit record has to be retrieved from all three bureaus; there is no way around that. So, what's the *truth* about inquiries and your credit score? It is true that if someone checks your credit it will cost you points, although it is likely not to cost you the number of points you may think. Typically, a single credit pull will have a minimal (1 to 5 point) impact on a credit score. Furthermore, under a new rule enacted in 2003, all credit pulls within a 30 day period for either an auto loan or mortgage are counted <u>as just one pull.</u> This provision is to allow people to shop around for the best interest rate without being penalized for doing so. Therefore, unless you are chronically applying for new credit month after month, the issue of inquires adversely impacting your credit score is not one about which you need to be very concerned.

Rapid Rescoring

Rapid rescoring is the latest buzz in the credit industry. My mortgage office was set up to do rapid rescores, although they are not as easy to get approved as people would like to believe. Rapid rescoring allows a credit grantor to correct an inaccuracy on a credit report and get a new credit score, based on the correction, usually within 24 hours. The rules on rapid rescoring are very strict and this strategy can only be used in very limited circumstances. In order to remove or update a negative item through rapid rescoring, you must have a letter on the letterhead of the creditor acknowledging the error. For example, if you have paid off a debt that is still showing, and you have a letter or invoice showing *Paid In Full*, you could likely get that item removed under rapid rescoring. The purpose of this is to provide people with a method of quickly resolving mistakes when time is limited (2 days before a real estate closing, etc...). Most mortgage brokers are set up to do rapid rescores for their clients when the situation warrants.

Reason Codes

Reason codes represent a more detailed breakdown of the factors that influence a given credit score. At the beginning of this report, I outlined the fact that all of your credit information is boiled down to a three digit credit score. Think of reason codes as subtotals that, combined, become your score. Don't get out a calculator and start adding together your reason codes - that is not how the scoring is arrived at. Through a very complicated algorithm, all of your credit activity is analyzed and a score is generated. Another way to think of reason codes is as the ingredients in a recipe: the cake (your score) is the final outcome, and the reason codes are the individual ingredients (egg, butter, flour, etc...).

Not all consumer-accessible credit reports include reason codes, but virtually all credit reports accessed directly by a potential credit grantor *will*. You have every right to ask for a copy of your credit report the next time you are involved in a financing transaction with a credit-granting institution or company. Once you get your hands on the commercial version of your credit report, you will see your reason codes right next to each of your three credit scores.

Here is an example of what I might see:

Score 620   10   38   04

Reason codes are listed in the order that they are weighted into a specific credit report. In this case the first reason code is a 10. If you look at the reason code list provided in the following pages, you will see that a 10 indicates that the balances on revolving accounts are too high.

38 = Derogatory Public Record Item (such as a bankruptcy, foreclosure, judgment, or tax lien).

04 = Too Few Open National Accounts

Do a Google search and you can easily find an up to date reasons code list to make reference to.

Your Notes And Action Plan:

Credit Repair Letters

Sample Letters to Correct Credit Problems

Remove Unauthorized Credit Inquiries Sample Letter

Date

Your Name
Street Address
City, State Zip

Name of Credit Bureau
Street Address
City, State Zip

To: Customer Service

I have recently received a copy of my credit report as maintained by your reporting agency. The report I received contains credit inquiries that I never authorized. I request that the following inquiries be deleted immediately:

(List the name of the creditor here)
(List the creditor code here)
(List the account number here)
(Describe the inaccuracy here)

After you have made the appropriate deletions, please send me an updated copy of my credit report.

Sincerely,

(Your signature here)
(Your typed name here)
(Your social Security number here)
(Your date of birth here)

Sample letter for disputing inaccurate information

To: Customer Service Dept.

I have reviewed a copy of my credit file as it is maintained by your organization. Unfortunately, I have discovered that some of the information contained therein is inaccurate. The purpose of this letter is to ask that you initiate an investigation immediately regarding this inaccurate information. The inaccurate entries are as follows:

List here the name of the creditor who is the source of the entry.

List the creditor code here.

List the account number here.

Describe the inaccuracy here.

In accordance with the provisions of the Fair Credit Reporting Act, I expect to be advised of the results of this investigation within 30 days. Furthermore, in accordance with the same Act, I expect that the information will be removed if it cannot be verified. Once your investigation is complete, please send me an updated copy of my credit report.

Thank you for your assistance in this matter.

Sincerely,

(Your signature here)
(Your typed name here)
(Your social Security number here)
(Your date of birth here)

Remove 7-Year-Old Information From Your Credit Report Sample Letter

To: Customer Service Dept.

I have recently received a copy of my credit report as maintained by your reporting agency. The report I received contains information that is more than seven years old. Per the Fair Credit Reporting Act, I understand that you are responsible for deleting this information from my record. Please delete the following:

(List the name of the creditor here)
(List the creditor code here)
(List the account number here)

After your investigation is completed, please send me an updated copy of my credit report.

Sincerely,

(Your signature here)
(Your typed name here)
(Your social Security number here)
(Your date of birth here)

Sample Letter For Disputing Negative Information That Is Accurate And Not Yet Outdated

To: Customer Service Dept.

I have reviewed a copy of my credit file as it is maintained by your organization. My copy of this credit file contains the following entries which I would like to have re-verified at once:

List here the name of the creditor who is the source of the entry.

List the creditor code here.

List the account number here.

In accordance with the provisions of the Fair Credit Reporting Act, I expect to be advised of the results of this investigation within 30 days. Furthermore, in accordance with the same Act, I expect that the information will be removed if it cannot be verified. Once your investigation is complete, please send me an updated copy of my credit report.

Thank you for your assistance in this matter.

Sincerely,

(Your signature here)
(Your typed name here)
(Your social Security number here)
(Your date of birth here)

Sample Cease And Desist Letter

To: Customer Service Dept.

In accordance with the provisions of the Fair Debt Collection Practices Act, I am requesting that your firm no longer contact me by phone. Please contact me only in writing by mail, regarding any business matters regarding my account (s) with your firm.

Thank you for your assistance in this matter.

Sincerely,

(Your signature here)
(Your typed name here)
(Your social Security number here)
(Your date of birth here)